INSTANT PIANO AND GUITAR

ONE AND TWO CHORD SONGS

Public domain songs compiled by Angela Taylor

KDP Publishing 2024
All rights reserved

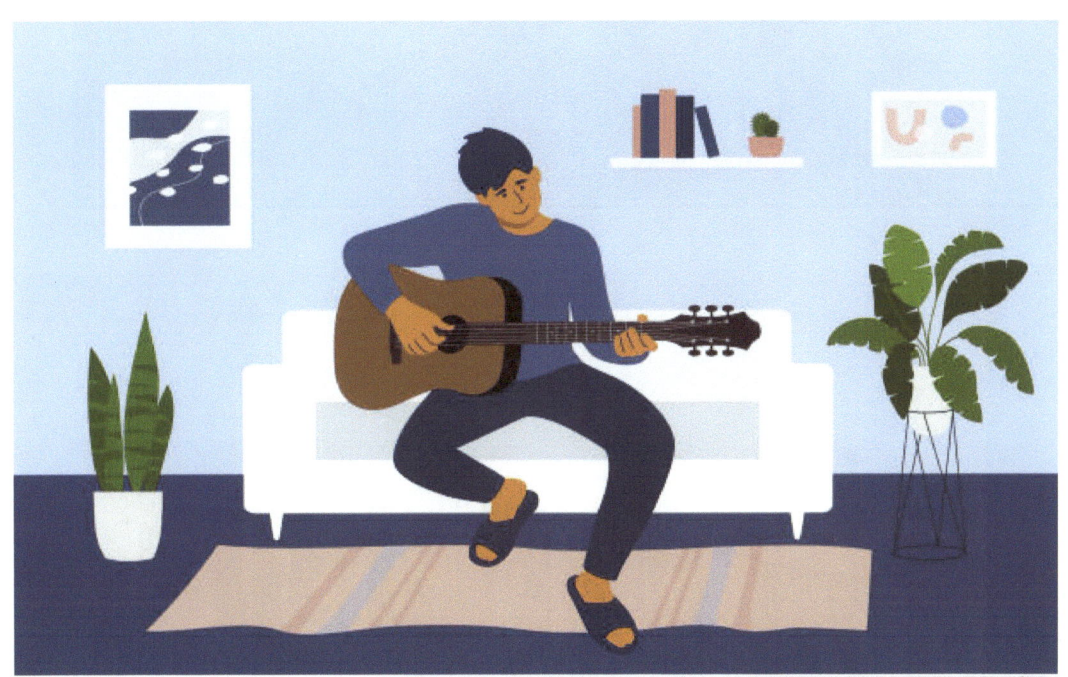

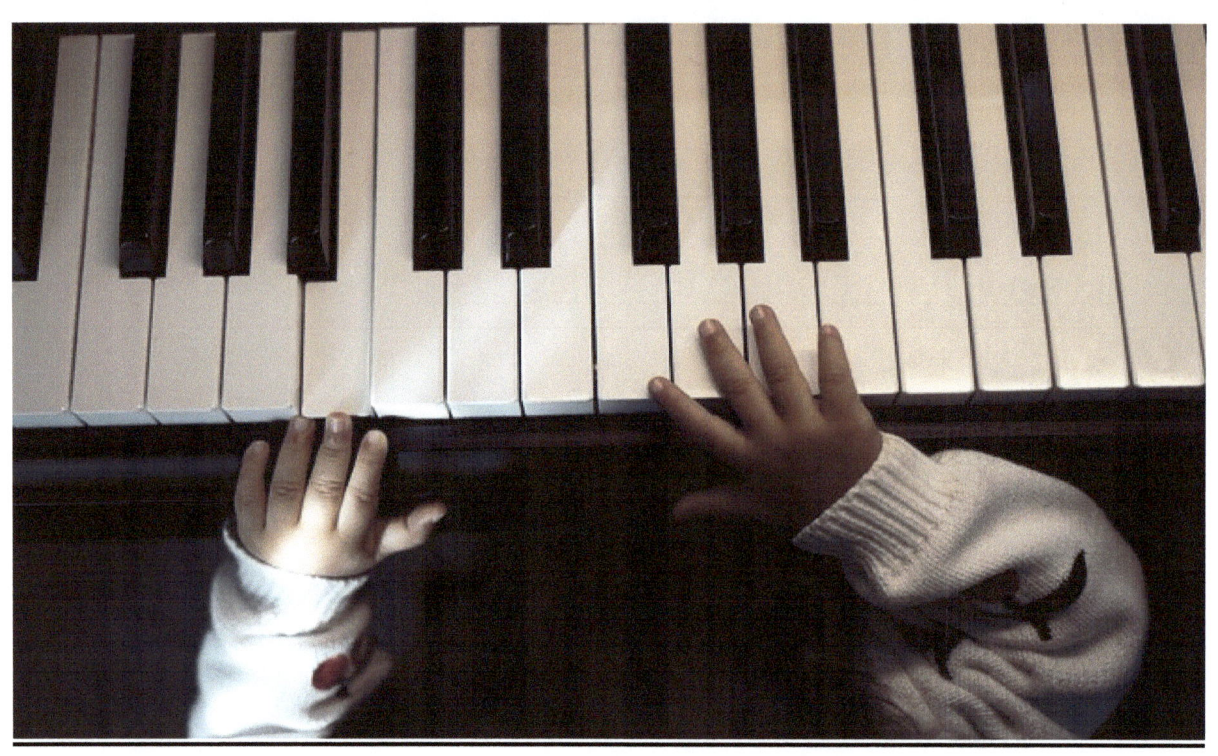
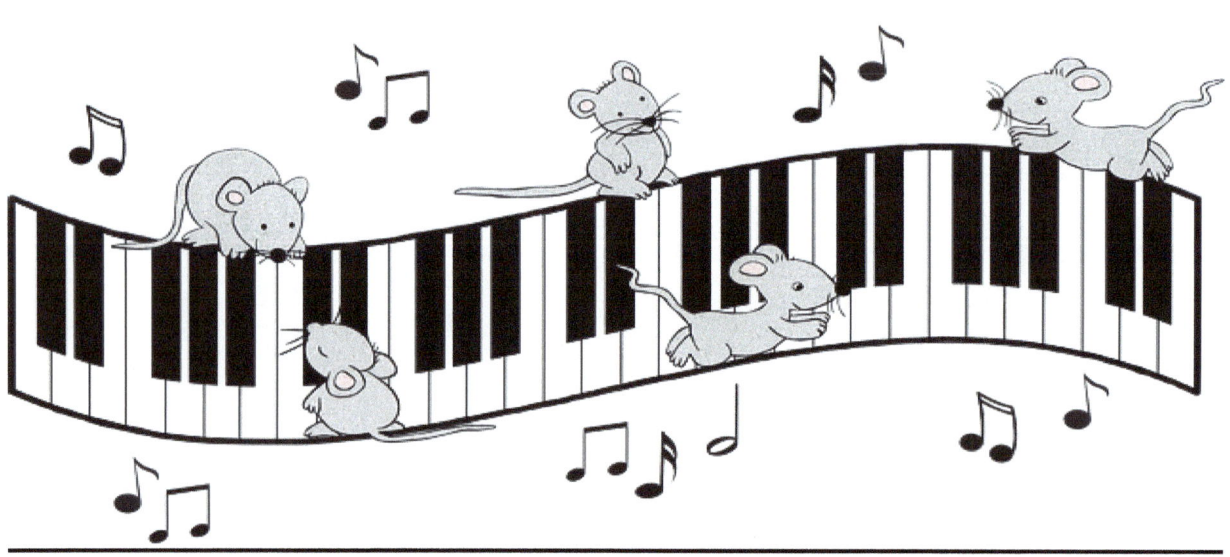

TABLE OF CONTENTS

One chord songs — G CHORD

Row Row Row Your Boat	page 10
The Farmer in the Dell	12
Are You Sleeping = Frere Jacques	13

Two chord songs (G, C) and (G, D)

G and C chords
Hokey Pokey	14
Jambalaya	15
London Bridges	16
Skip to my Lou	17

G and D chords songs
Buffalo Gals	18
Shorten Bread	19

BONUS SONG....use G, C, D chords — 20
- Another Day to Love

CHORDS YOU WILL USE, for Piano and Guitar

G

C

D

STRUMMING GUITAR…..

On all guitar songs, strum DOWN, DOWN, DOWN, DOWN motion

G

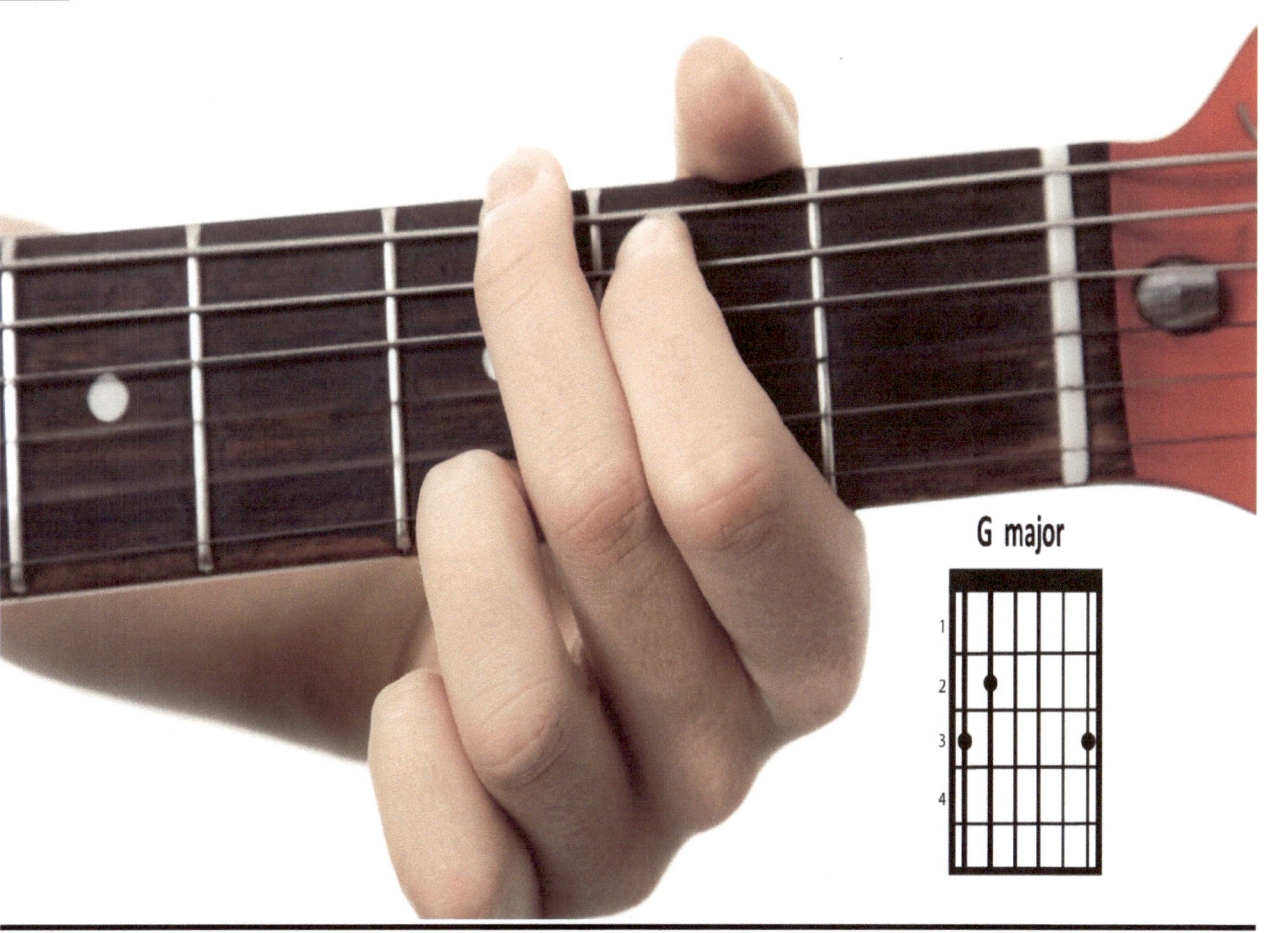

G major

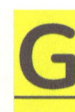

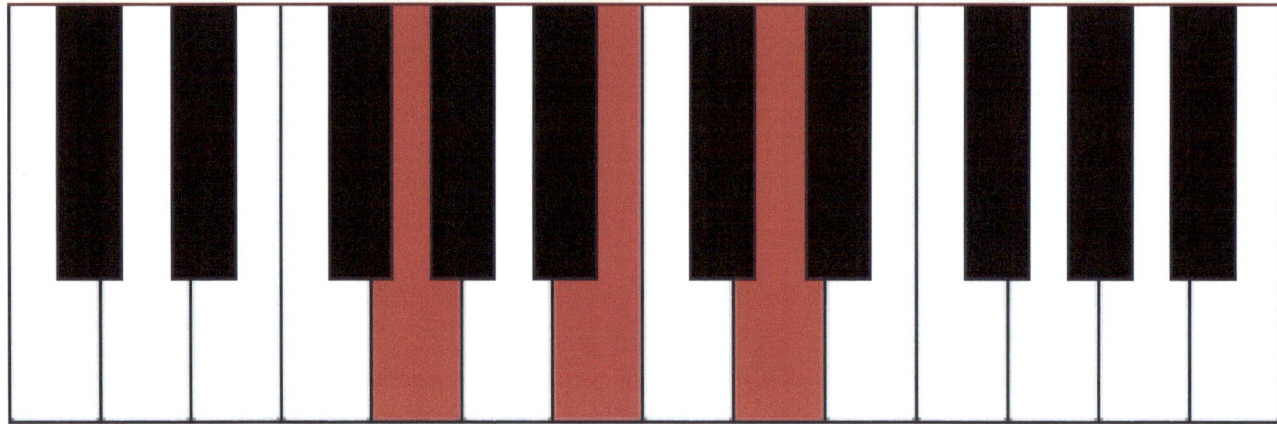

(in RED) G - B - D create the G CHORD

If you only use your **Left hand**: 5-3-1 (5th finger, 3rd finger, 1st finger)

If you only use your **Right hand**: 1-3-5 (1st finger, 3rd finger, 5th finger)

D

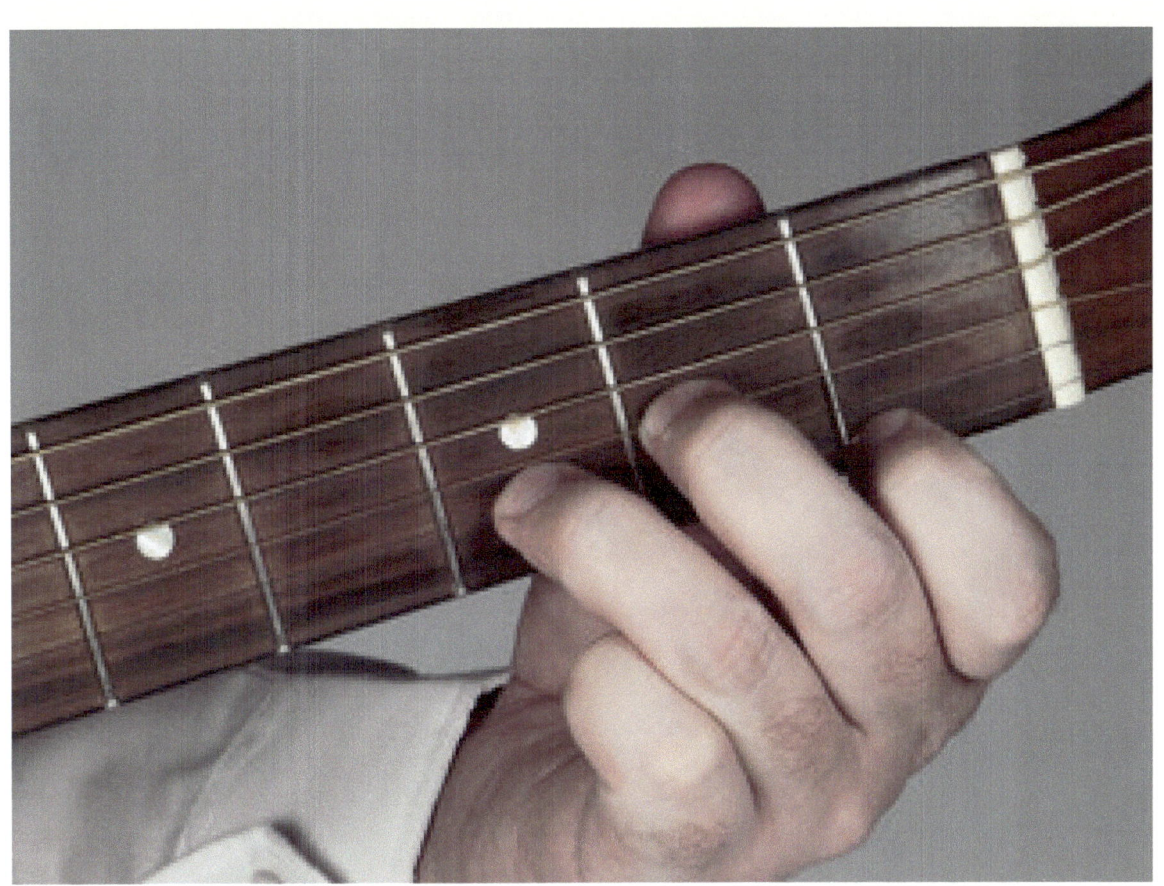

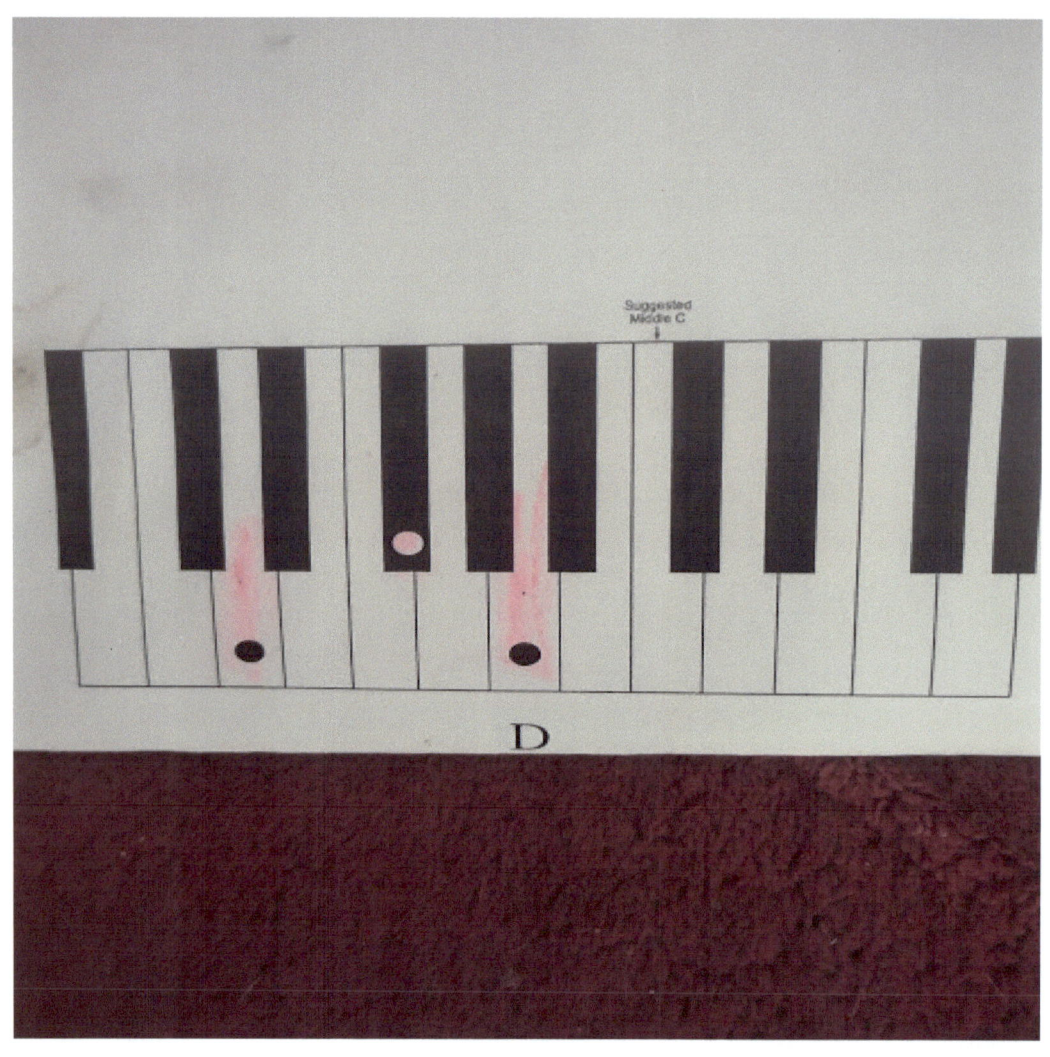

D

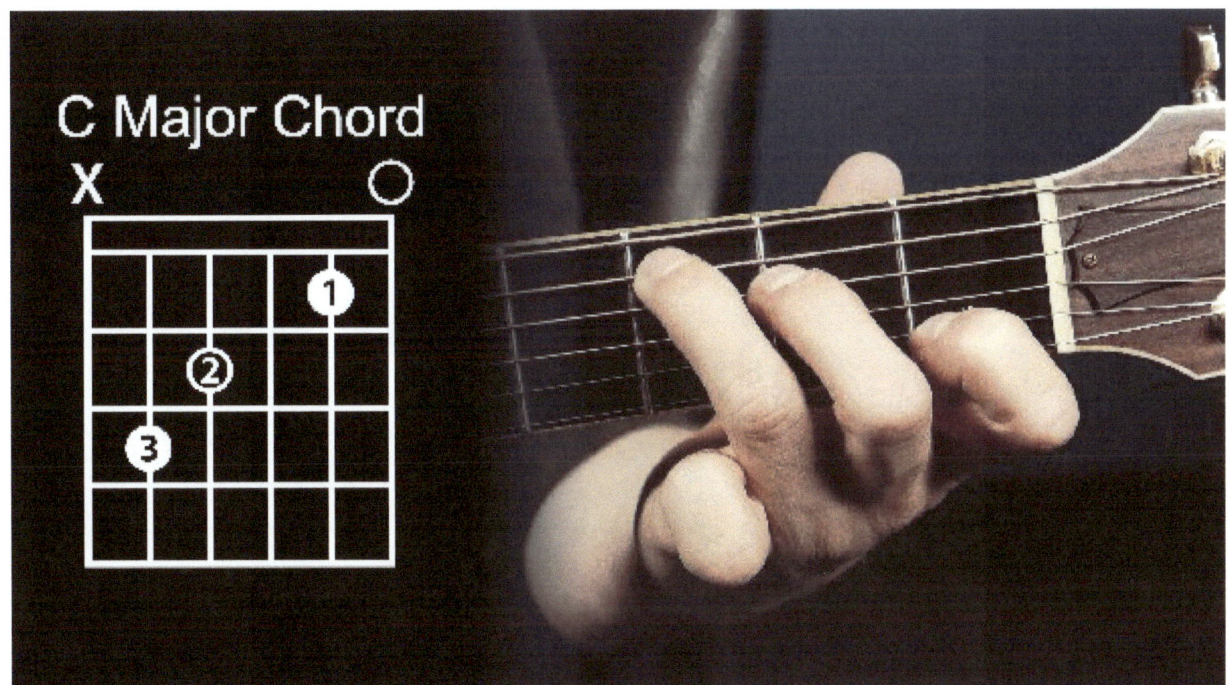

C

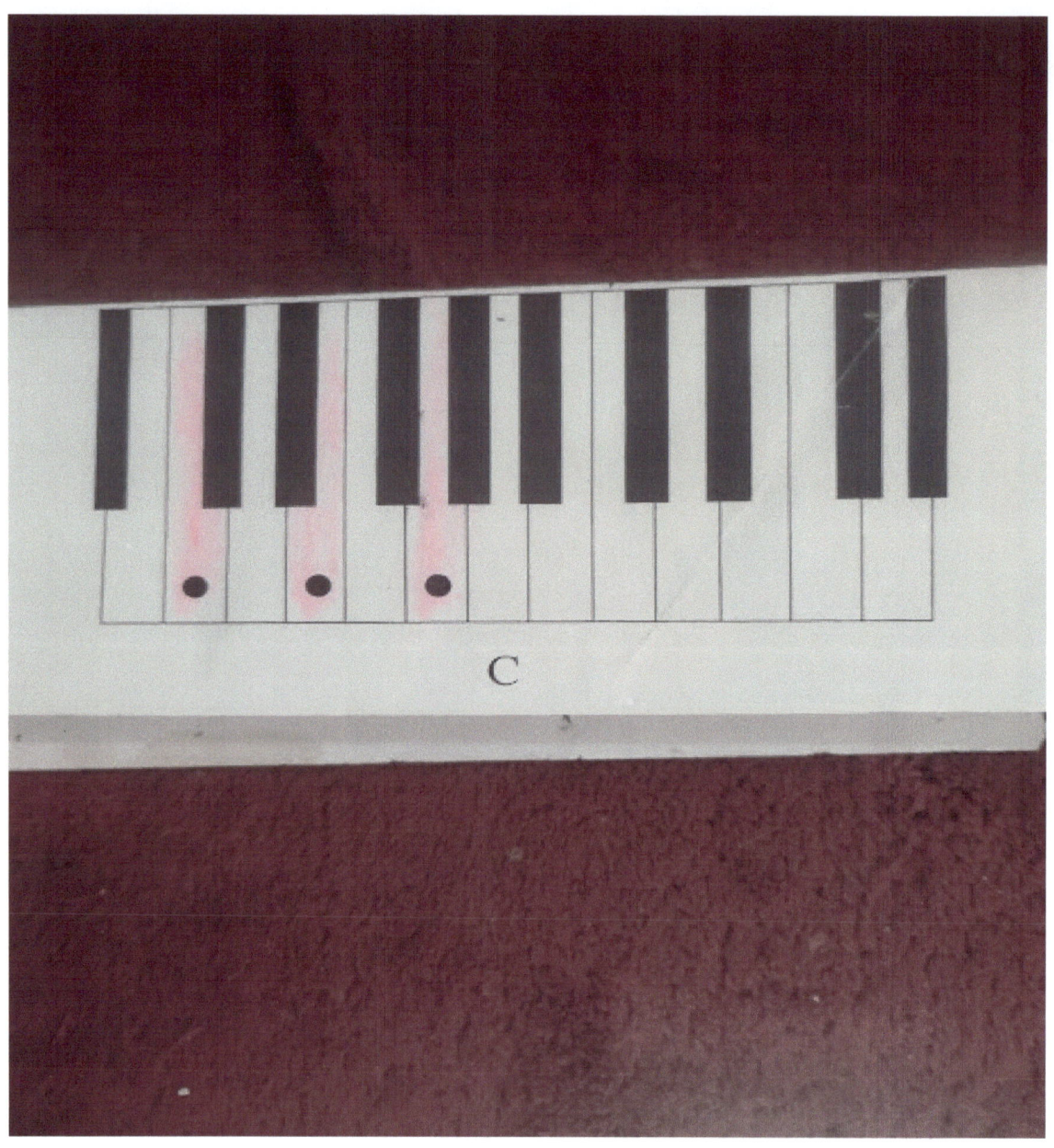

C

ROW ROW ROW YOUR BOAT   G CHORD

G
ROW ROW ROW YOUR BOAT

ROW ROW ROW YOUR BOAT

GENTLY DOWN THE STREAM

MERRILY MERRILY MERRILY

LIFE IS BUT A DREAM

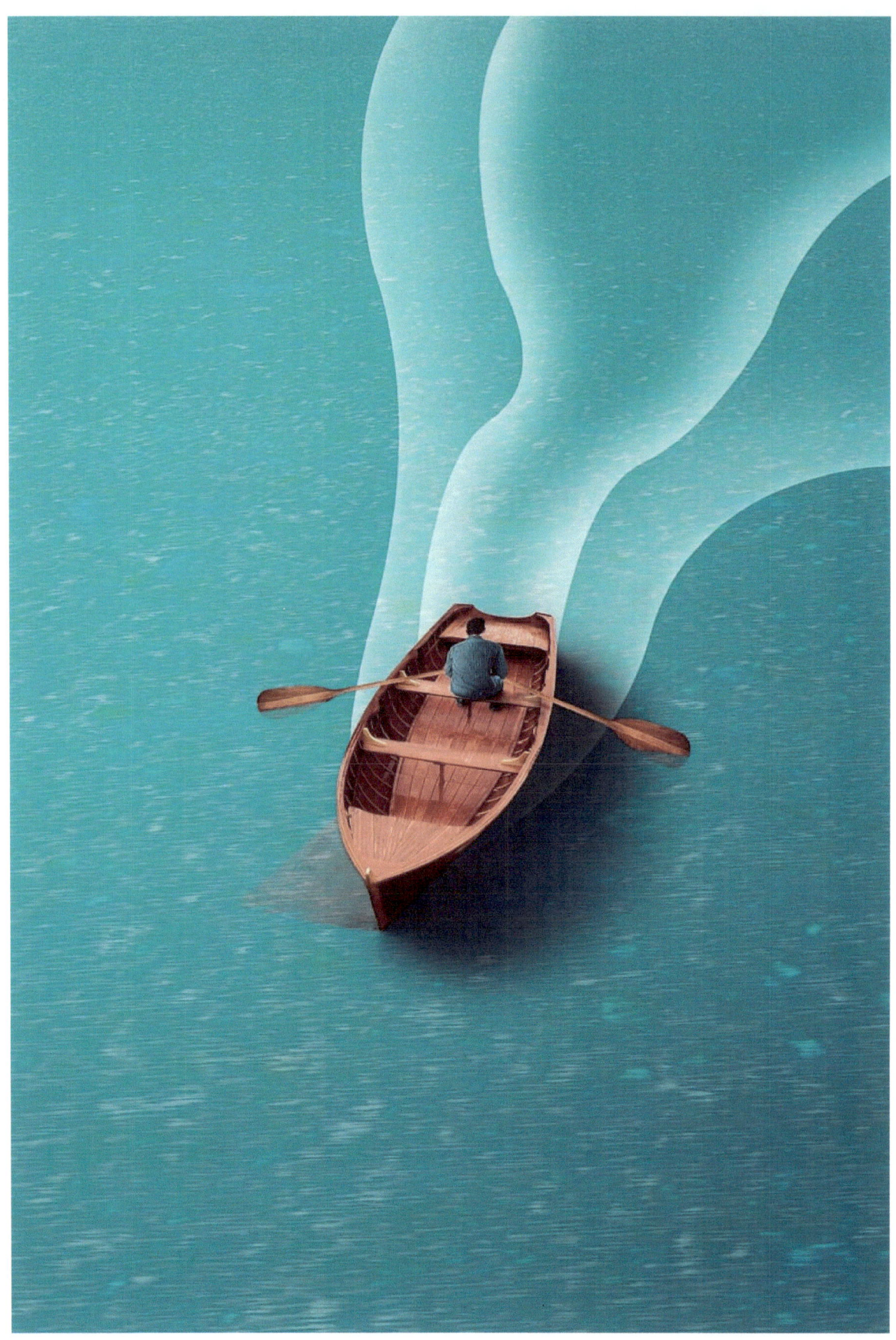

THE FARMER IN THE DELL — G CHORD

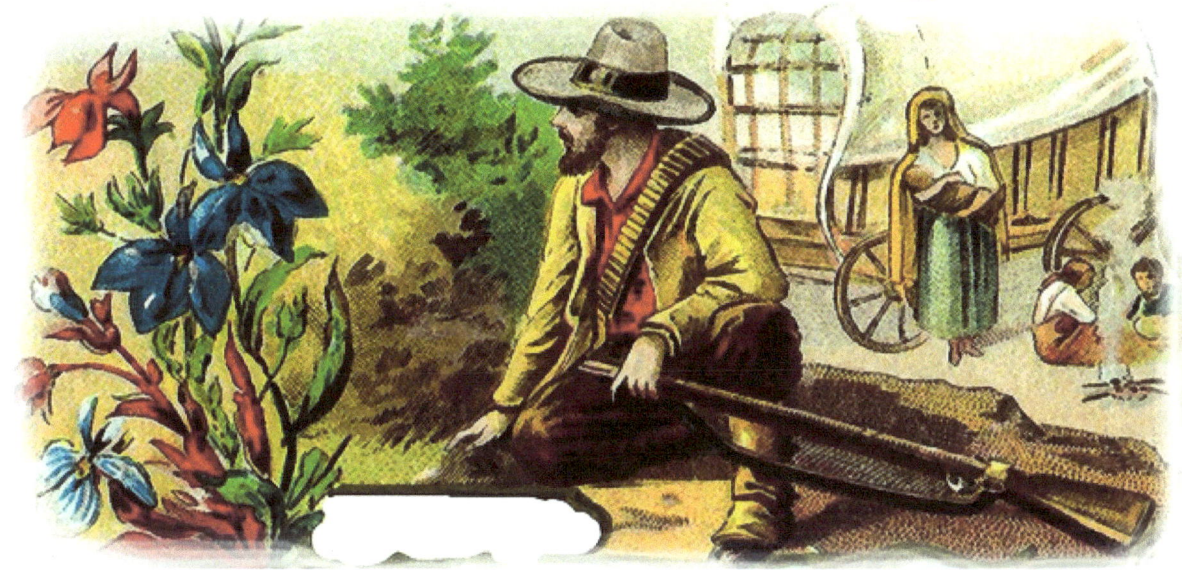

G

The farmer in the dell

The farmer in the dell

Hi-ho, the derry-o

The farmer in the dell

The farmer takes a wife

The farmer takes a wife

Hi-ho, the derry-o

The farmer takes a wife

ARE YOU SLEEPING, FRERE JACQUES — G CHORD

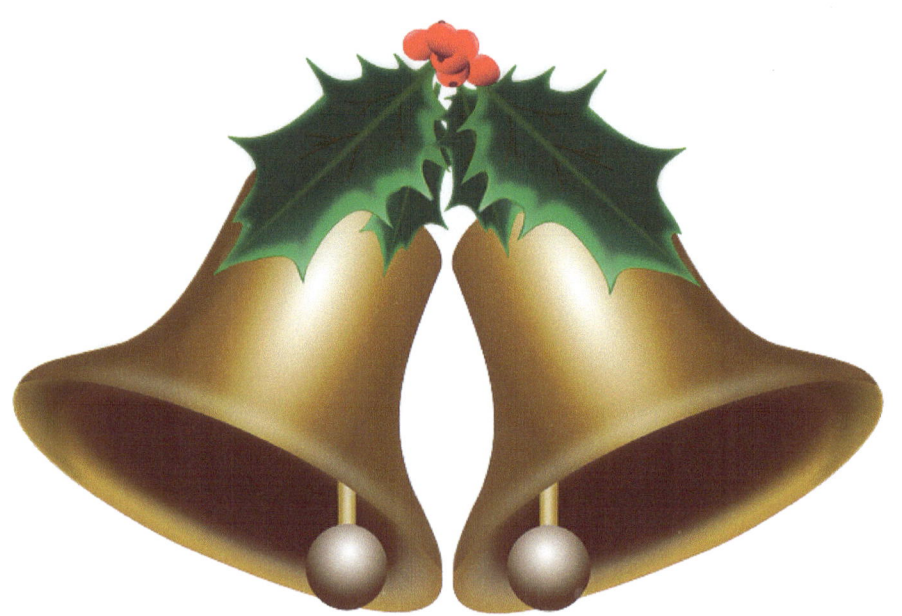

G
Are you sleeping? Are you sleeping?
Brother John, Brother John,
Morning bells are ringing! Morning bells are ringing!
Ding, ding, dong. Ding, ding, dong.

FRENCH VERSION OF ARE YOU SLEEPING

G

Frère Jacques, Frère Jacques

Dormez-vous? Dormez-vous?

Sonnez les matines, Sonnez les matines

Ding Ding Dong. Ding Ding Dong

HOKEY POKEY   C AND G CHORDS

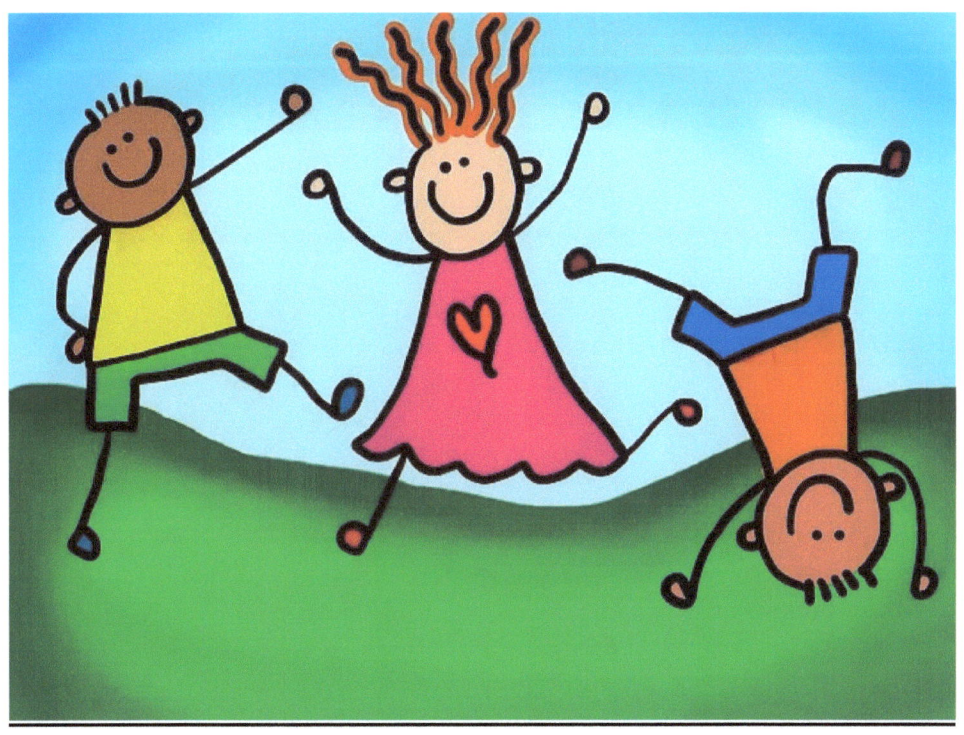

C
You put your right foot in
You put your right foot out
You put your right foot in

     G
And you shake it all about
You do the hokey pokey and you turn yourself around
            C
That's what it's all about!

JAMBALAYA — C AND G CHORDS

Goodbye, Joe, me gotta go, me oh my oh
                                                       C
Me gotta go, pole the pirogue down the bayou
                                   G
My Yvonne, the sweetest one, me oh my oh
                                        C
Son of a gun, we'll have big fun on the bayou

                                                G
Jambalaya and a crawfish pie and Filé gumbo
                                                   C
Cause tonight I'm gonna see my ma cher amio
                                        G
Pick guitar, fill fruit jar and be gay-o

Son of a gun, we'll have big fun on the bayou

                                         G
Thibodaux, Fontaineaux, the place is buzzin'
                                  C
Kinfolk come to see Yvonne by the dozen
                                         G
We dress in style and go hog wild, me oh my oh
                                      C
Son of a gun, we'll have big fun on the bayou

LONDON BRIDGES FALLING DOWN C AND G CHORDS

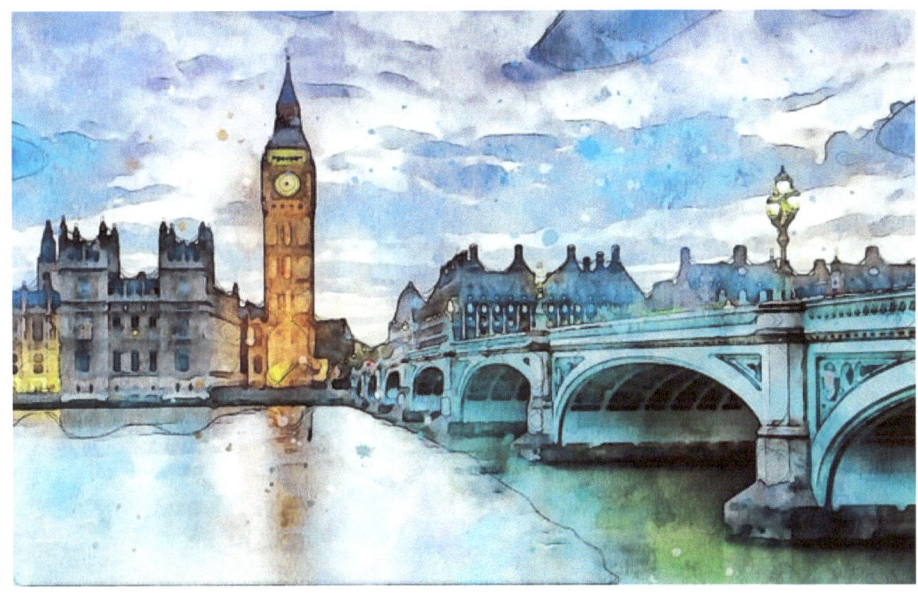

[C] London Bridge is falling down

[G] Falling down [C] falling down

[C] London Bridge is falling down

[G] My fair [C] lady

[C] Build it up with wood and clay

[G] Wood and clay [C] wood and clay

[C] Build it up with wood and clay

[G] My fair [C] lady

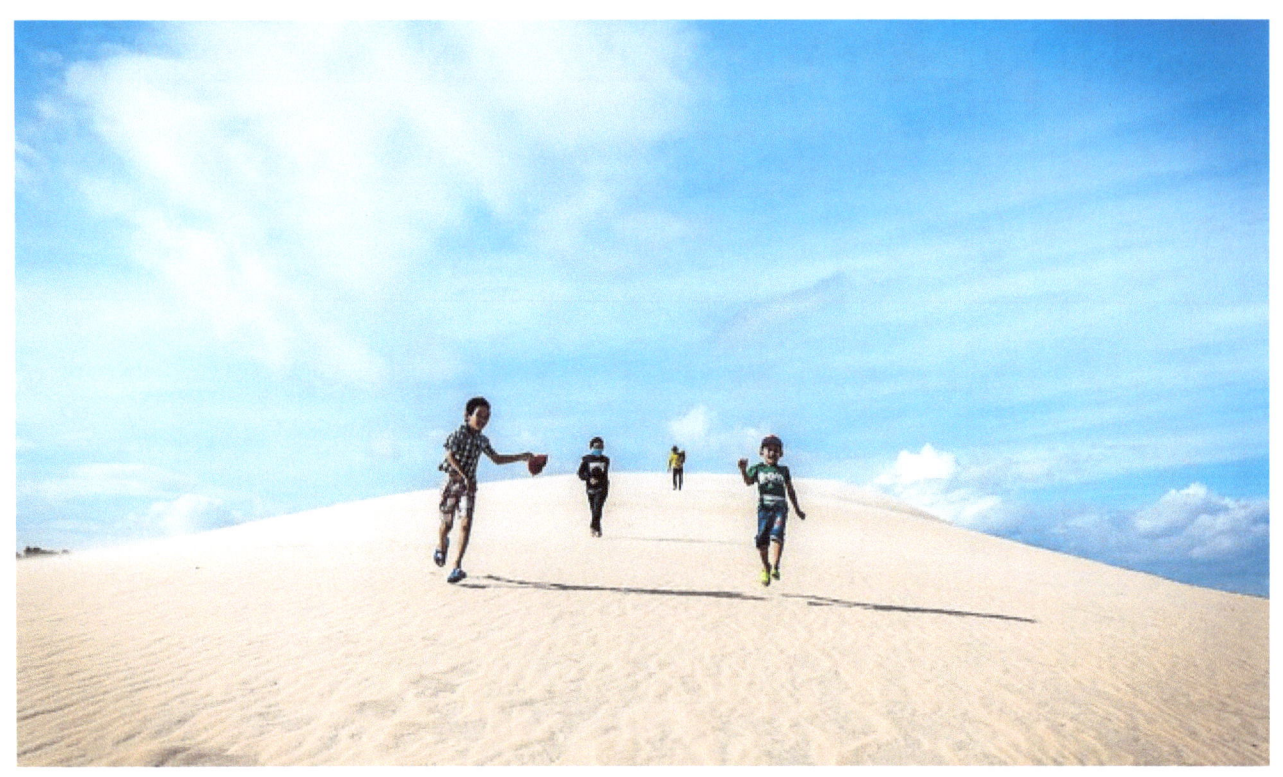

SKIP TO MY LOU   C AND G CHORDS

C
Skip, skip, skip to my Lou,
G
Skip, skip, skip to my Lou,
C
Skip, skip, skip to my Lou,
G   **C**
Skip to my Lou, my darlin'.

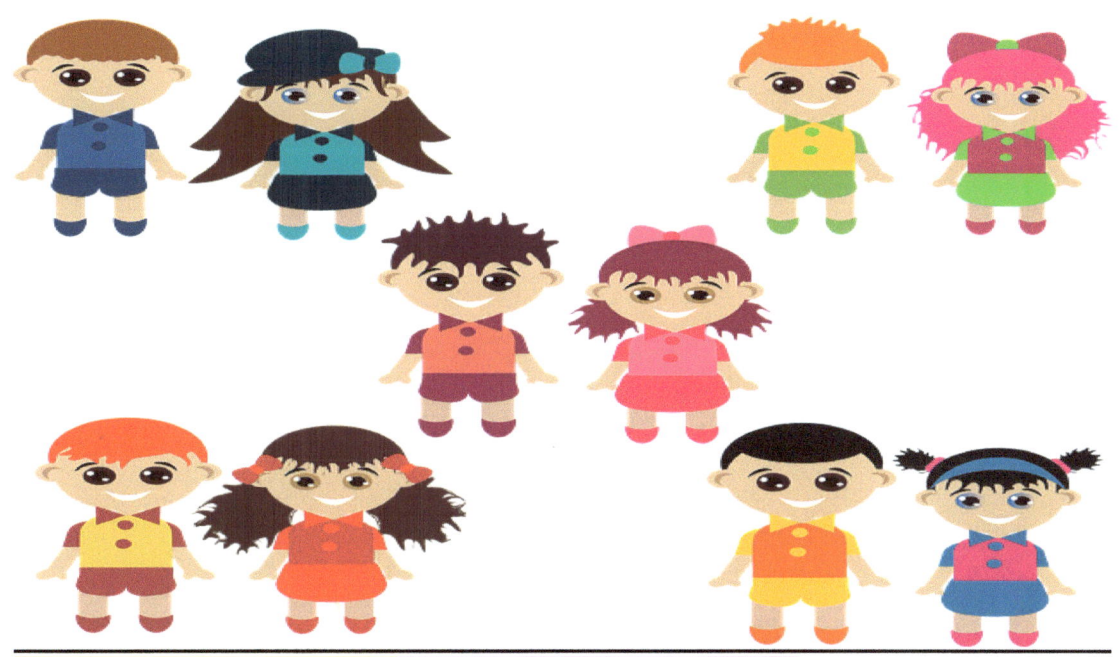

BUFFALO GALS C AND D CHORDS

G
As I was walking down the street,
D   G
Down the street, down the street,
G
A pretty little gal I chanced to meet,
D   G
Oh, she was so fair.

[Chorus]
G
Buffalo Gals, won't you come out tonight,
D   G
Come out tonight, come out tonight.
G
Buffalo Gals, won't you come out tonight
D   G
And dance by the light of the moon.

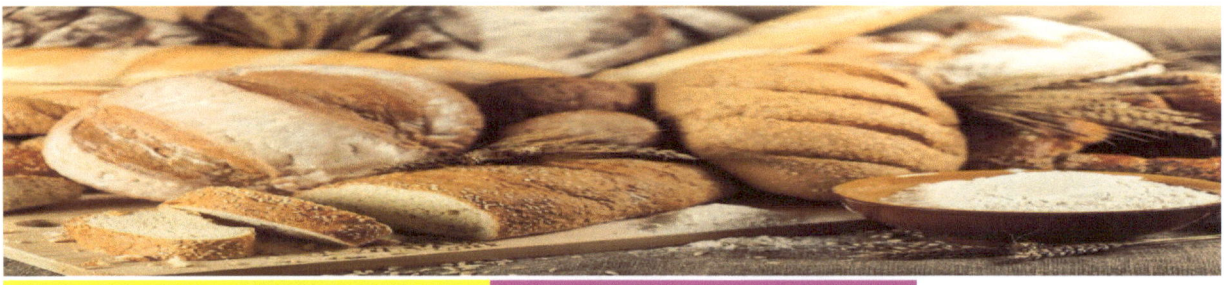

SHORTEN BREAD — C AND D CHORDS

G
Mama's little baby loves short'nin', short'nin',

                     D
Mama's little baby loves short'nin' bread,

G
Mama's little baby loves short'nin', short'nin',

                     D
Mama's little baby loves short'nin' bread.

G
Put on the skillet, slip on the lid,

                     D
Mama's gonna make a little shortnin' bread.

G
That ain't all she's gonna do,

                     D
Mama's gonna make a little coffee, too.

ANOTHER DAY TO LOVE   * G, C, D* chords

Here the song on …youtube.com, songbooksafari

```
G
OVER THE HILLS THE DAWN IS BREAKING
C              D
THROUGH THE SKY ABOVE
G
OVER THE EARTH THE DAY IS AWAKENING
C      D     G
ANOTHER DAY TO LOVE


G
SITTING UPON A GREEN GRASS HILLTOP
C              D
GAZING FROM ABOVE
G
I SEE THE BIRDS FLY TREE TO TREE TOP
C      D     G
ANOTHER DAY TO LOVE


C          G
LOVE, LOVE, COVERING THE WORLD IN LOVE

C      D     G
LOVE, LOVE, SPREADING EVERYWHERE


G
OVER THE EARTH THE MOON IS RISING
C              D
GLOWING FROM ABOVE
G
I HAD A DAY THAT WAS SO SUPRISING
C      D     G
```

ANOTHER DAY TO LOVE

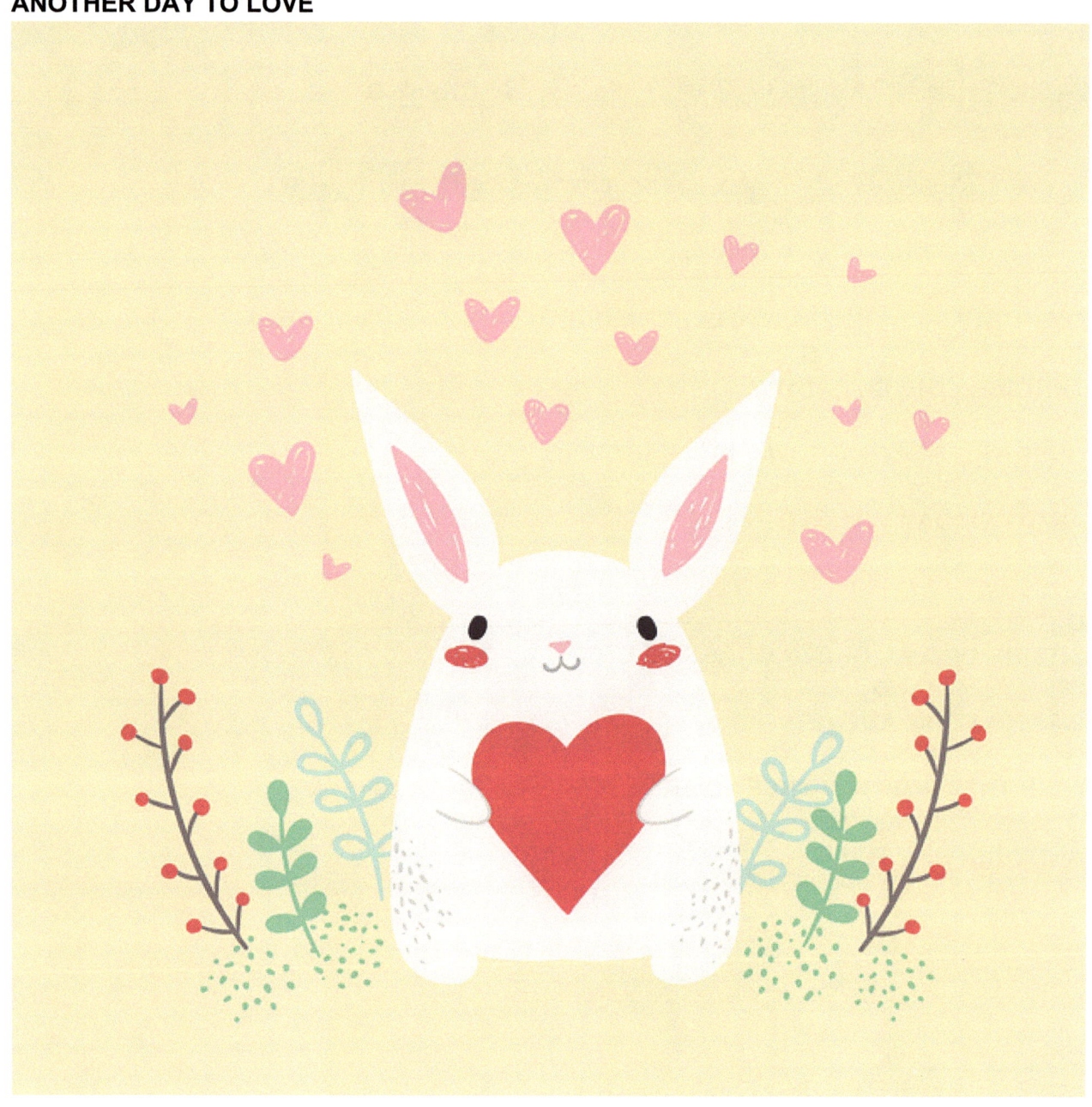

Angela Taylor - Author

Email: learnguitarasap@gmail.com

PUBLISHED BOOKS

Band Aide - how to book your band — Personhood Press

The Purple Bull — Creative House Press

The Purple Cat Ventures —-Creative House Press

Angels of Protection - Creative House Press

Cents of Humor - penny jokes

TUTOR/TEACHER (Bachelor of Science College Degree)

English/Reading/Language Arts And English as a Second Language (ESL)	Guitar Lessons (beginning) Art (drawing, crafts) (beginning) Math, elementary school

MUSIC (my bands) and (songwriter)

The BABY BOOMERS BAND was my oldies band I booked for many years and I wrote the BAND AIDE book about it all. I sing and play basic guitar. I was in a jazz band+spiritual band as well, and wrote songs for kids, jazz, pop, country, spiritual, etc., genres.

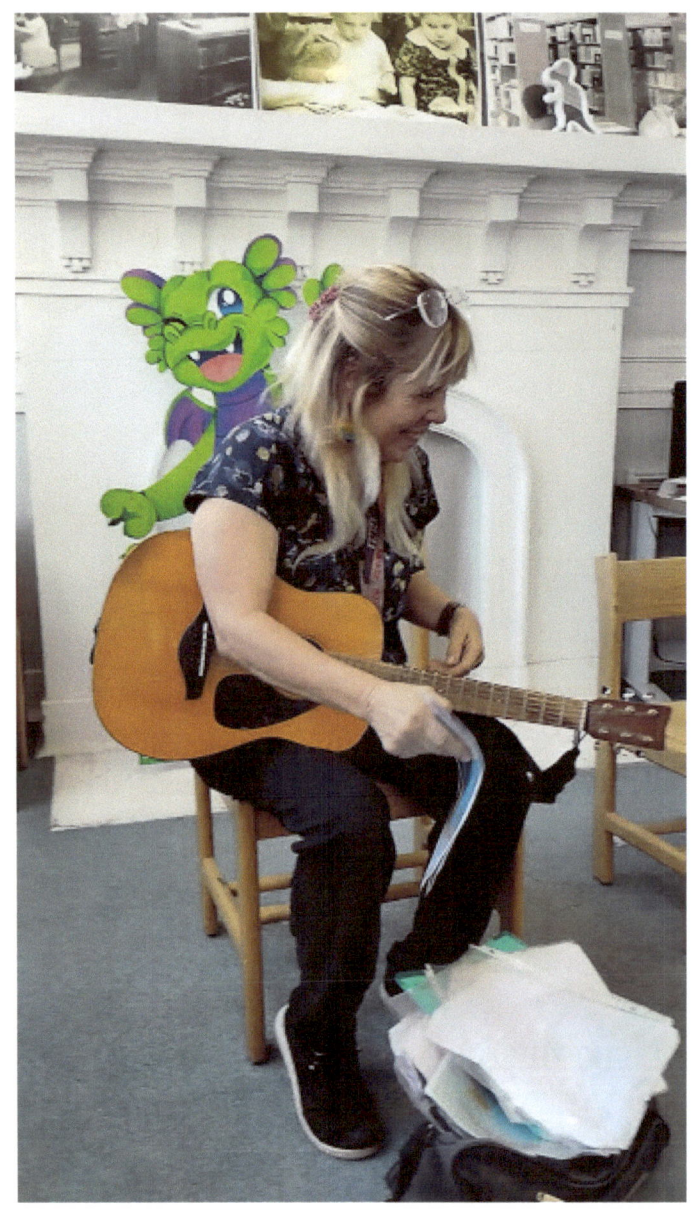

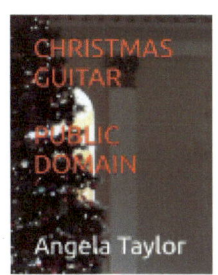

CHRISTMAS GUITAR PUBLIC DOMAIN

By Angela Taylor

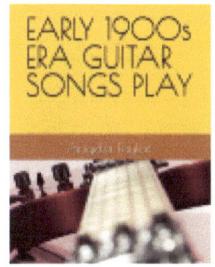

EARLY 1900s ERA GUITAR SONGS PLAY

By Angela Taylor

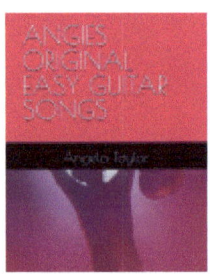

ANGIES ORIGINAL EASY GUITAR SONGS

By Angela T

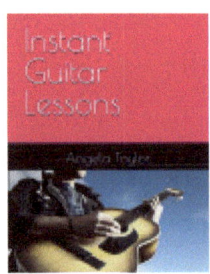

Instant Guitar Lessons

By Angela Taylor

FREE PIANO and GUITAR/ LESSONS ONLINE

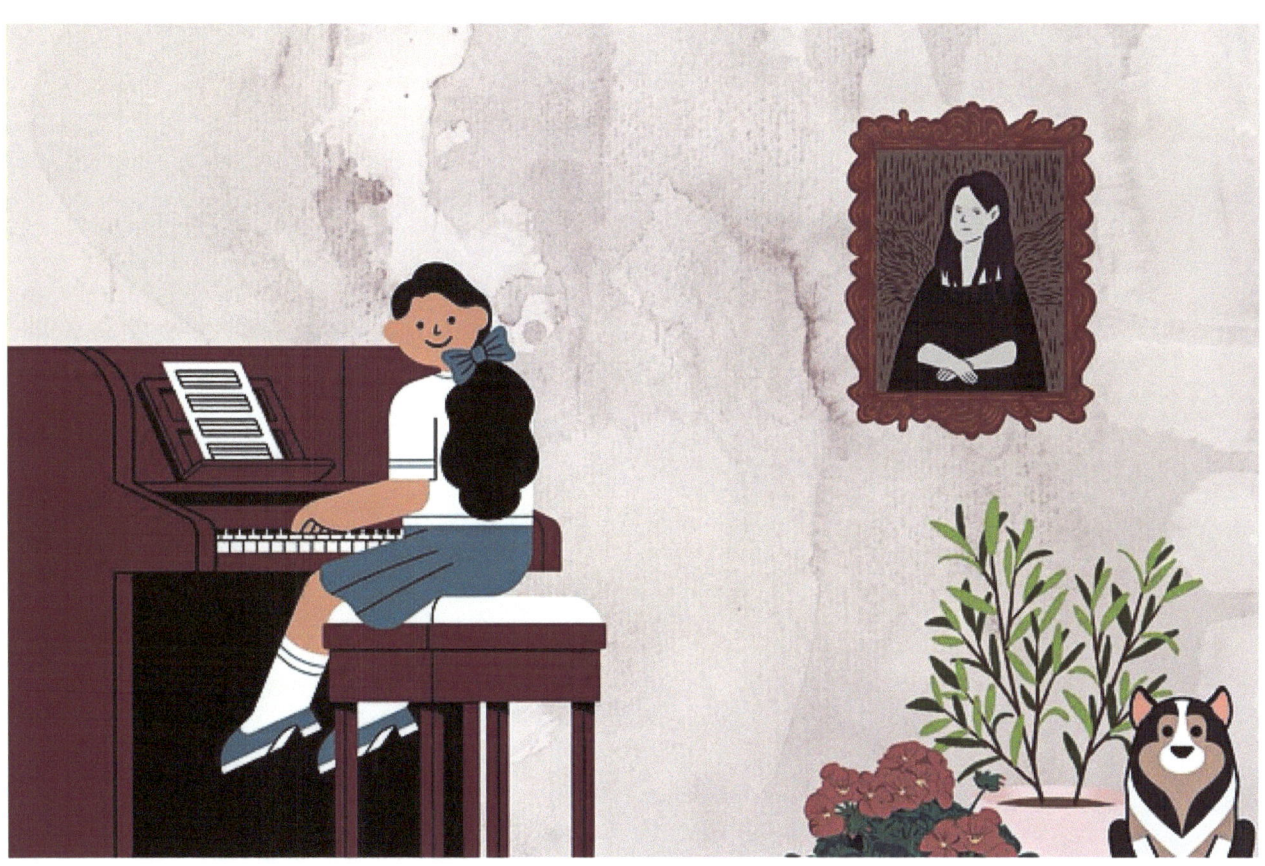

youtube.com
@songbooksafari

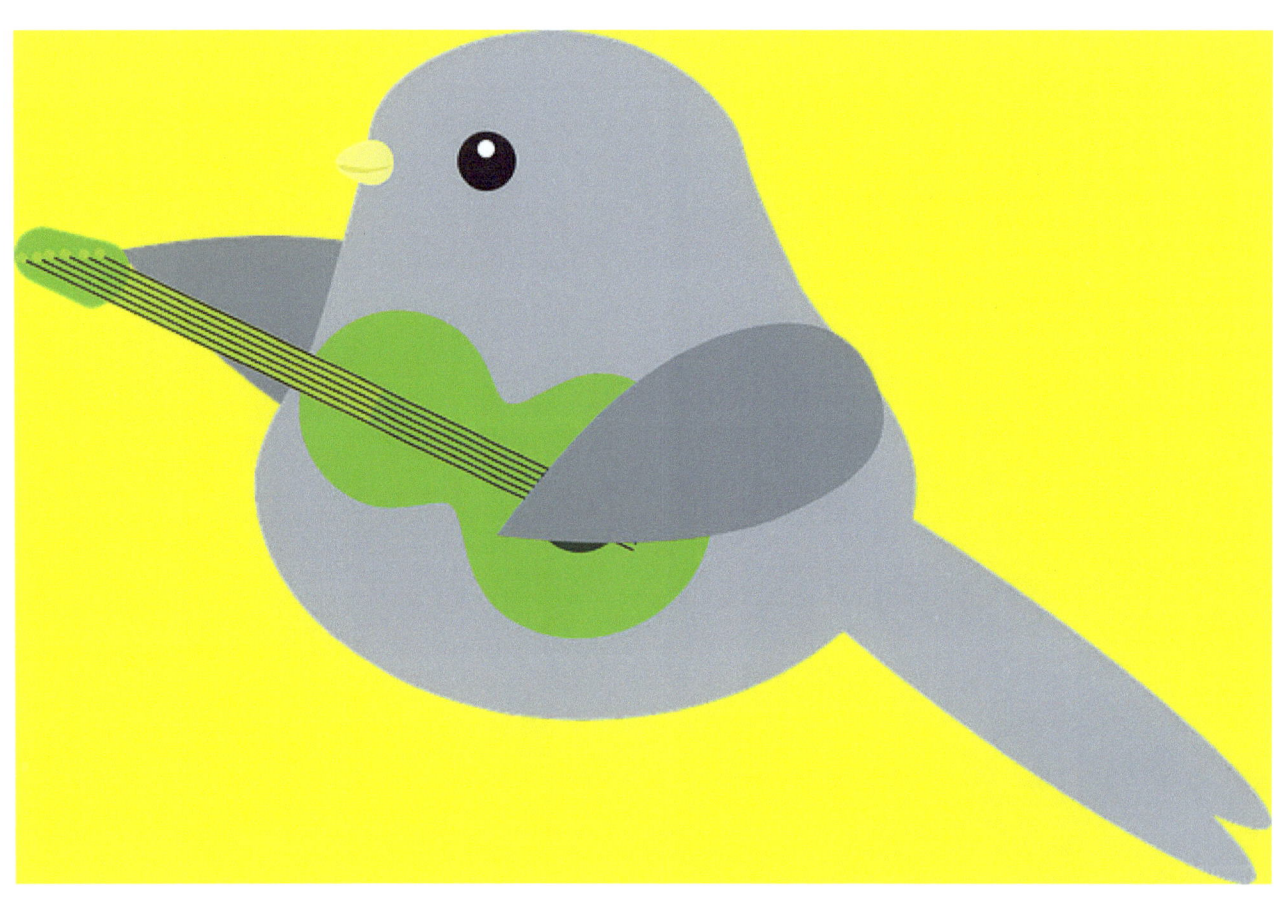